GW00385100

Vegetarian
Recipes
from the West Country

Margaret Wilson

Bossiney Books

CONTENTS

This reprint 2015
Second edition first published 2004 by
Bossiney Books Ltd, 33 Queens Drive, Ilkley LS29 9QW
www.bossineybooks.com
Copyright © 2000, 2004 Margaret Wilson
All rights reserved
ISBN 978-1-899383-70-0
Cover photography by Andrew Besley

Printed in Great Britain by R Booth Limited, Penryn, Cornwall

INTRODUCTION

After the success of my *Devonshire Cookbook*, the heat was on to produce a second book, this time concentrating on my regional vegetarian recipes which we enjoyed at home and offered in the restaurant.

The challenge was not too great, as here in the West Country we have an abundance of local produce which means that cooking is an absolute delight. The simplicity of the fresh ingredients is the key to my selected recipes. They are quick, easy and fun to make and, above all, delicious to eat.

The vegetarian cheeses I use come from Somerset, Devon and Cornwall – we are very lucky to have excellent specialist cheese shops in Exeter, Tavistock and Topsham which sell a wide selection over the counter. They also have a mail order service, so anyone wanting advice about cheese, or to buy local specialities, can contact Country Cheeses on-line, or at Market Road, Behind Pannier Market, Tavistock, Devon PL19 0BW, telephone (01822) 615035. And of course many supermarkets now sell local cheeses. Or you might prefer to substitute your own favourites.

Many people are also quite fanatical about buying Cornish new potatoes at the start of the season, as they say they have the best flavour of any 'teddies' anywhere. Again, it's obviously down to personal preference and availability at your local shops. But if you haven't tried them before and you get the chance, do experiment – you might be pleasantly surprised.

Finally, I've included a syllabub recipe which calls for a sweet cider. Cider is another West Country gem, and there are numerous small farmhouse cider makers spread all over the counties who are each producing their own distinctive blends. Try to get hold of some of their 'golden liquor' if you can – it'll make all the difference!

Margaret Wilson

SOUPS

Cream of asparagus soup

(serves 4)

450 g (1lb) fresh asparagus
75 g (3oz) butter
1.2 litres (2 pints) vegetable stock (see page 31)
1 medium onion, chopped
1 clove garlic, crushed
2 medium potatoes, chopped small and very fine
150 ml (¼ pint) single cream

Prepare the asparagus by chopping off the stalks (keep the woody parts and trimmings for your stock) and cutting up the tender parts.

Melt the butter in a pan over a low heat. Sauté the onions, potato and garlic until soft and without colour. This takes about 15 minutes with the lid on – keep checking to make sure they don't go brown. Then add the prepared asparagus and the stock, and cook for 15 minutes or until the asparagus is soft. Tip into a blender and blend until very smooth. Pour in the cream, check the seasoning and serve.

Cream of cauliflower and blue cheese soup

(serves 4)
2 small cauliflowers
75 ml (3 fl oz) clarified butter
1 medium onion
1 crushed clove of garlic
2 medium floury potatoes, finely chopped
1.2 litres (2 pints) cold water or vegetable stock (see page 31)
75g (3 oz) Somerset or Devonshire blue cheese, grated
150 ml (¼ pint) single cream

Prepare the cauliflowers: discard all the leaves, but keep the stalks, and wash and chop. Heat the butter in a large pan and cook the onion until it is soft and without colour. Add the crushed garlic, potato and cauliflower, and sauté gently together for 5 minutes, stirring all the time and not allowing the mixture to brown. Add the stock and simmer for 20 minutes or until all the vegetables are cooked. Take from the heat and blend until creamy. Stir in the grated blue cheese and cream, season to taste, and serve.

Courgette and sorrel soup
(serves 6)

225 g (8 oz) potatoes, finely chopped
225 g (8 oz) onions, finely chopped
1 kg (2 lb 2 oz) courgettes, washed and diced
2 tbsp freshly chopped tarragon
75 g (3 oz) shredded sorrel leaves
2 litres (3^1/$_2$ pints) good vegetable stock (see page 31)
50 g (2 oz) butter
75 ml (3 fl oz) double cream
1 clove garlic, chopped, and seasoning

Put the chopped potatoes and a little salt in a large saucepan, and just cover them with cold water. Bring them to the boil and blanch for 2 minutes. Strain in a colander.

In another large saucepan carefully melt the butter on a low heat. Gently sauté the onions and garlic until soft and transparent, then add the courgettes and cook together for 5 minutes. Add the potatoes and the stock, and cook for a further 10 minutes or until the potatoes are soft.

Transfer the mixture to a blender with the sorrel and tarragon, and blast until it's very smooth. Pour in the cream and check the seasoning. The soup is now ready to serve. Decorate with a swirl of double cream and finely chopped tarragon.

MAIN COURSES

Winter vegetable stew with herby dumplings
(serves 4)

For the stew
    225 g (8 oz) carrots, peeled and diced
    225 g (8 oz) parsnips, peeled and diced
    225 g (8 oz) swede, peeled and diced
    450 g (1 lb) potatoes
    1 large onion, chopped
    110 g (4 oz) red lentils
    2.4 litres (4 pints) vegetable stock (see page 31)
    1 level tsp salt
    milled black pepper

In a large saucepan place all the vegetables, lentils and stock, and bring to the boil. Turn down the heat and simmer for 40 minutes, giving the occasional stir as the lentils may stick a little. Check the seasoning and add the dumplings.

For the herby dumplings
    110 g (4 oz) self-raising flour
    milled pepper
    pinch of salt
    50 g (2 oz) vegetarian suet
    $1/2$ tsp freshly chopped thyme
    $1/2$ tsp freshly chopped parsley
    150 ml ($1/4$ pint) cold water

Put all the dry ingredients into a bowl and mix with the cold water to form a soft ball. Divide into smaller balls, drop them into the stew and cover with a lid. Cook for about 10 minutes, during which time the dumplings will rise and double in size. When they have reached this stage the stew is ready for serving.

Devon farmhouse cheddar, bramley apple and pasta bake
(serves 6)

I use North Devon cheddar cheese in this recipe because it has a good strong flavour which enhances the apple and the pasta.

225 g (8 oz) leeks, sliced and cooked
225 g (8 oz) apple purée
225 g (8 oz) farmhouse cheddar cheese, grated
175 g (6 oz) fresh pasta
2 tbsp fresh tarragon, chopped
25 g (1 oz) butter
25 g (1 oz) flour
425 ml (3/4 pint) milk
150 ml (1/4 pint) cream
1/4 tsp cinnamon
1/4 tsp salt
freshly milled black pepper

Place the cooked leeks, apple purée and pasta in a bowl, and add the cinnamon, tarragon, salt and pepper, and cheese. Give the mixture a good stir until all the ingredients are well integrated.

Next, melt the butter in a pan over a low heat. Add the flour and cook for 1 minute. Then pour in the milk a little at a time, stirring continually. Finally, add the cream, give a firm whisk and fold the sauce into the vegetables and pasta.

Transfer to an oven-proof dish, check the seasoning and bake at 200°C/400°F/gas mark 6 for 30 minutes or until golden brown.

As an attractive alternative, melt 50g (2 oz) butter in a pan over a low heat and add 225g (4 oz) baked wholemeal bread crumbs with a crushed clove of garlic. Cook for 2 minutes and sprinkle over the top of your bake 5 minutes before it's ready to take out of the oven.

Layered vegetable loaf

(makes approximately 10 slices)

175 g (6 oz) spinach leaves
110 g (4 oz) carrots, cut into baton shapes
225 g (8 oz) broccoli florets
225 g (8 oz) cauliflower florets
6 button mushrooms
4 asparagus spears
25 g (1 oz) butter
425 ml ($^3/_4$ pint) double cream
1 clove garlic, crushed
5 eggs, beaten
$^1/_2$ tsp salt
milled black pepper
175 g (6 oz) potato, puréed
200 g (7 oz) Cornish pepper cream cheese

Wash and blanch the spinach for 1 minute. Plunge into cold water and remove any stalks. Bring a pan of salted water to the boil and this time blanch the cauliflower, broccoli, carrots and asparagus for a few minutes. Again plunge everything into cold water and drain.

Sauté the mushrooms in the butter with the crushed garlic until soft but not overdone.

Oil a 1 kg (2 lb) loaf tin and line with the spinach leaves. Whisk the eggs, cream, peppered cheese and potato purée together with the seasoning. Then place a layer of this mixture in the tin, followed by some of each of the vegetables. Repeat until everything has been used. Enclose with spinach leaves and cover with parchment paper.

Wrap the whole thing in tin foil and stand in a baking tin of water (bain marie). Cook in the oven at 180⁰C/350⁰F/gas mark 4 for 2 hours. Remove and leave to cool, then refrigerate and serve cold.

Spicy veggi burger
(makes 8)

110 g (4 oz) cooked chick peas
110 g (4 oz) red kidney beans
1 tsp chilli powder
1 clove garlic, crushed
1 large onion, finely chopped
1 green and 1 red pepper, finely chopped
1 tsp tomato purée
110 g (4 oz) wholemeal breadcrumbs
2 eggs
salt
25 g (1 oz) butter
50 g (2 oz) wholemeal flour
1 tbsp olive oil

Heat the butter in a pan over a low heat and sauté the onions, garlic and peppers for about 10 minutes until soft. Place in a bowl and leave to cool.

Meanwhile purée half the chickpeas and half the red kidney beans, and roughly chop the rest. Add all the ingredients, except the flour, to the cooled onions and peppers. Give a good stir until everything sticks together.

Rub some flour on your hands to help shape the burgers and to make them brown evenly. Divide the mixture into eight 5 cm (2 in) rounds.

Heat the oil in a shallow pan and cook them for 2 minutes on each side. Or, if you prefer, you can cook them in the oven at 190°C/375°F/gas mark 5 for 15–20 minutes or until they are brown on both sides.

Another alternative is to barbecue them at medium heat for 3–4 minutes each side.

West Country pasty

(makes 4)

For the pastry
  450 g (1 lb) plain flour
  225 g (8 oz) butter
  1 tbsp mustard powder
  pinch each of cayenne pepper and salt
  275 ml (^{1}/$_2$ pint) water

Rub the butter into the sieved dry ingredients. Add the water to form a dough, wrap in cling film and chill for 20 minutes.

For the filling
  225 g (8 oz) creamed potatoes
  225 g (8 oz) blanched cauliflower
  225 g (8 oz) blanched broccoli
  110 g (4 oz) Godminster cheddar cheese, grated
  seasoning
  25 g (1 oz) butter
  3 tbsp milk
  1 egg, beaten

In salted boiling water blanch the cauliflower and broccoli, and cook the potatoes thoroughly. Drain and cream the potatoes with the butter. Then add the grated cheese and the chopped blanched vegetables, and season to taste. Leave to cool for approximately 30 minutes.

Roll out the pastry and cut out four circles (tea plate size), each roughly 13 cm (5 in) in diameter. Brush around the edges with milk, and divide the vegetable mixture between them – place in the centre of each, then bring the edges of the pastry together, and crimp or press together firmly with your thumb and forefinger. Brush with egg glaze and cook at 200ºC/400ºF/gas mark 6 on a baking tray lined with parchment paper for 40 minutes or until golden brown.

Spring onion and Cornish goat's cheese tart
(serves 6-8)

For the pastry
   225 g (8 oz) wholemeal flour
   100 g (4 oz) butter, cubed   1 egg yolk
   pinch of salt   2 tbsp cold water

Put the flour and salt into a bowl and rub in the cubed butter. Add the egg yolk and cold water. Wrap in cling film and put into the fridge for 25 minutes. Meanwhile preheat the oven to 190°C/ 380°F/gas mark 6. Grease a 23 cm (9 in) flan tin and then line it after rolling out the chilled pastry. Bake blind (by covering with parchment and filling with baking beans) for 20–25 minutes. While the base is cooking, prepare the filling.

For the filling
   4 spring onions, finely chopped
   1 clove garlic, crushed and 1 tsp English mustard
   2 tbsp fresh herbs (parsley, chives and tarragon)
   225 g (8 oz) soft Cornish goat's cheese
   4 eggs, beaten
   175 ml (8 fl oz) double cream
   salt and cayenne pepper for seasoning

In a large mixing bowl beat together everything except the cheese and spring onions. Take the flan case from the oven and carefully remove the parchment and beans. Make sure the pastry is sufficiently cooked, remembering it has to go back into the oven again with the filling. But if it still looks a bit soggy in the middle, return it to the oven and keep an eye on it for another 3–5 minutes.

Spread the goat's cheese over the case bottom and sprinkle on the spring onions. Then add the egg and cream mixture. Reduce the oven temperature to 180°C/360°F/gas mark 5, and bake for 30 minutes. The tart should turn golden brown.

Savoury vegetable summer pudding
(serves 4-6)

This is delicious served with spicy tomato sauce – see page 29.

1.5 litre (2^1/$_2$ pint) pudding basin
8 slices stale white or brown bread, crusts removed
1 red pepper and 1 yellow pepper, quartered, de-seeded,
      grilled, skinned and chopped
1 medium red onion, thinly sliced
1 garlic clove, crushed
225 g (8 oz) courgettes, diced
225 g (8 oz) tomatoes, blanched, skinned and chopped
seasoning
6 fresh basil leaves, chopped
mild olive oil

Brush the basin with olive oil and cut the bread into appropriate shapes to line it – not forgetting a piece for the lid!

Brush the peppers with oil and pop them under the grill to burn off the skin. Put in an airtight bag when cool and the skins should peel off easily. Blanch the tomatoes, then skin and chop them.

Next, heat a frying pan with a tablespoon of oil and place the sliced onion in it. Cook for around 5 minutes until soft and transparent. Add the seasoning, crushed garlic, chopped courgettes, tomatoes and peppers, and give a good stir. Check the seasoning and add the chopped basil leaves.

Finally, put everything into the prepared pudding basin, top it with the bread lid, and brush with olive oil. Bake in the oven at 190⁰C/375⁰F/gas mark 5 for 30 minutes.

Wild field mushroom kedgeree

(serves 6)

75 g (3 oz) butter
1 medium onion, thinly sliced
450 g (1 lb) long grain rice
1 carrot, finely chopped
1 leek, finely chopped
1 litre (2 pints) vegetable stock, see page 31
1 pinch saffron
225 g (8 oz) wild field mushrooms, sliced
450 ml (3/4 pint) single cream
1/2 tsp curry paste
3 eggs
pinch of salt
3 tbsp chopped parsley

Pour the vegetable stock into a saucepan, bring to the boil and add the salt, washed rice and saffron. Boil without a lid for 15 minutes or until all the stock has been absorbed. Add the cream to the cooked rice and heat gently for 2 minutes, stirring all the time.

Melt the butter in a large pan and cook the onion, carrot, leek and lastly the sliced mushrooms gently for about 10 minutes until soft and without colour. Transfer the rice to a warmed serving dish, then add the vegetable mixture, chopped parsley and curry paste. Stir well.

While the rice is cooking, bring some water to the boil in a small sauccpan. Put the eggs in and boil for 10 minutes. Take off the heat and immerse the eggs in cold water. Peel and cut them into quarters, arrange them on top of the kedgeree, and serve.

Kale and West Country cream cheese roll

I often use this vegetarian roll for a finger buffet, as it's very colourful and tastes delicious.

110 g (8 oz) freshly cut kale
50 g (2 oz) butter
4 eggs, separated
50 g (2 oz) Vulscoombe goat's cheese
seasoning

Preheat the oven to 190°C/375°F/gas mark 5 and line a 20x30 cm (8x12 in) Swiss roll tin with baking parchment.

Prepare the kale by washing it, taking off any tough stalks and draining the leaves in a colander. Melt 25g (1 oz) butter in a saucepan, put in the kale, cover with a lid and cook gently for 5 minutes. Give it a stir after 2 minutes, and make sure you don't overcook – the kale should keep its bright green colour. Then take off the heat, add the remaining butter and leave to cool for a few minutes.

Transfer the kale to a food processor or blender and chop for 30 seconds. Then put it in a mixing bowl, beat in the egg yolks and fold in the grated goat's cheese. Whisk the egg whites until they form soft peaks but are not too 'stiff' (if you overbeat them, the roll will take on a heavier texture).

Using a metal spoon, fold in a little of the egg white to relax the mixture, and gradually fold in the rest very gently, giving it plenty of air to make the roll light.

Spread evenly onto the lined Swiss roll tin and bake in the centre of the oven for 10 minutes or until firm. Remove from the oven and turn out onto a sheet of parchment paper.

Take off the lining paper and roll from the longest side while still hot. Leave to cool on a wire rack.

For the filling
1 each green, red and yellow peppers, de-seeded and chopped
1 red onion, peeled, sliced and chopped
1 clove garlic, crushed
110 g (4 oz) Cornish black pepper cream cheese
2 tbsp olive oil and 2 tbsp mayonnaise (see page 30)

Heat the oil in a pan and gently cook the onions, peppers and garlic together until soft and without colour. Place in a bowl to cool. In another bowl cream the pepper cream cheese and mayonnaise together and then mix in the cold cooked ingredients. Gently unroll the kale base, fill it with the mixture, then roll it back up tightly from the longest side, trim the ends, and serve.

Onion, fennel and red pepper tarts
(makes 8 individual tarts)

1 large onion, finely chopped
1 red pepper, de-seeded and chopped
50 g (2 oz) button mushrooms, sliced
1 fennel bulb, finely chopped
275 ml (1/2 pint) double cream
3 eggs, beaten
50 g (2 oz) butter
50 g (2 oz) Cornish Garland cheese, grated
salt and freshly milled black pepper
8 individual pastry cases, baked blind (see page 11)

Melt the butter in a pan over a medium heat, making sure it doesn't brown. Sauté the onions, fennel and red pepper for about 7 minutes until soft. Then add the mushrooms and cook for a further 3 minutes. In a mixing bowl beat the eggs, cream and cheese together, and add seasoning. Put the vegetables in the mixture and stir well. Divide between each pastry case (10 cm/4 in wide and 4 cm/1½ in deep), and bake in the oven at 190°C/375°F/gas mark 5 for 20–25 minutes.

Individual double cheese soufflés

(makes 4 individual soufflés)

I make this tasty recipe with Tagon gruyère-style and Somerset or Devon blue cheeses.

50 g (2 oz) butter
50 g (2 oz) plain flour
75 g (3 oz) Somerset or Devon blue cheese, grated
75 g (3 oz) Tagon gruyère-style cheese, grated
4 egg yolks
250 ml (8 fl oz) milk
salt and cayenne pepper
7 egg whites
1 tbsp clarified butter, for brushing the dishes

Preheat the oven to 190°C/375°F/gas mark 5. You will need a baking tray – put it in the oven to warm – and four soufflé dishes 10 cm (4 in) in diameter and 5 cm (2 in) high.

Brush each of the soufflé dishes well with the clarified butter. Melt the rest of the butter in a pan over a low heat, add the flour, mix thoroughly and cook for 1 minute. Then gradually add the milk, stirring all the time.

When all the milk has been absorbed, take off the heat and cool slightly for 10 minutes. Next, beat in the egg yolks, gruyère and Somerset/Devon blue cheeses, and season to taste. Whisk the egg whites until they form soft peaks and very gently fold into the mixture.

Fill each dish to the top, place onto the hot tray and bake for 12–15 minutes or until they are golden brown and firmly risen

Devon carrot, parsnip, tomato and hazelnut pâté

For this recipe the pâté is baked in puff pastry and served with an onion and red wine sauce. It is easy to make, can be prepared the day before and is excellent at Christmas.

For the pâté
    2 tbsp olive oil (mild)
    1 large onion
    2 cloves garlic, finely chopped
    450 g (1 lb) fresh tomatoes, blanched, peeled and chopped
    175 g (6 oz) hazelnuts, finely chopped
    110 g (4 oz) each grated carrot and grated parsnip
    2 tbsp fresh tarragon, chopped
    1 egg
    1 level tsp salt
    milled black pepper
    1 x 450 g (1 lb) loaf tin, greased and lined with parchment

Heat the oil in a saucepan and cook the onion and garlic for 3–5 minutes on a low heat until soft and without colour. Add the carrot, parsnip, tarragon and tomatoes, and cook for a further 10 minutes. Take off the heat and allow to cool for 20 minutes. Then beat in the egg and the nuts, and check the seasoning. Press into a lined loaf tin and refrigerate for 2 hours to firm up the pâté.

For the puff pastry (this recipe makes 450 g (1 lb) of pastry)
    200 g (7 oz) butter, cubed   225 g (8 oz) plain flour
    1 tsp salt   3-4 tbsp ice cold water

Sieve the flour and salt into a bowl. Make a well in the centre and add 110 g (4 oz) butter cut into small cubes. Rub it in quickly and not too finely, squashing it through your finger tips. Pour the water in carefully and press the mixture together until it forms a soft dough. Knead gently into a ball, wrap in cling film and chill for 30 minutes.

On a lightly floured, cold surface (a marble slab is ideal for this) roll your pastry into a rectangle shape 1 cm (1/2 in) thick. Cover two thirds of it with the remaining cubes of butter. Fold the uncovered third to the centre, and then bring the opposite side on top so that all the butter is enclosed completely. Wrap in cling film and chill for a further 45 minutes.

Then roll the pastry into a rectangle once again – roll from the longest side. Fold it in, as before, and refrigerate for 20 minutes. Repeat this last stage. Your pastry is now ready to use.

Roll the pastry out into a rectangle (approximately 35x25 cm/14x10 in) on a cool floured surface. Take the pâté out of the fridge, turn it out of the loaf tin and place it in the centre of the pastry. Egg wash the edges and wrap the pâté into a neat parcel shape. Next, line a baking tray with parchment paper and place the 'pâté in pastry' (*pâté en croute*) onto it, making sure any pastry seam is tucked underneath. Egg wash the loaf evenly all over, and then make some pastry leaves with the trimmings. Egg wash these, and bake the whole in the oven at 200°C/400°F/gas mark 6 for 1 1/4 hours. While it is cooking, make the sauce.

For the onion and red wine sauce
  50 g (2 oz) butter
  1 large onion, finely chopped
  1 clove garlic, crushed
  1 tsp caster sugar
  425 ml (3/4 pint) red wine
  275 ml (1/2 pint) vegetable stock (see page 31)
  1 tbsp tomato purée
  seasoning
  2 tbsp fresh tarragon, chopped
  50 g (2 oz) plain flour

Melt the butter in a saucepan and add the onion. Cook slowly for about 15–20 minutes until the onion is brown and beginning to caramelise. Add the caster sugar and garlic, stir and cook for 2 minutes. Mix in the flour and tomato purée, and continue cooking for a further 2 minutes, stirring all the time.

Pour in a little of the vegetable stock and stir well to make sure it is well incorporated into the mixture. Repeat until all the liquid has been used and then simmer for 5 minutes without a lid, by which stage you should have the consistency of a sauce. Season and serve.

Home-made fresh basil and egg pasta

  2 litres (3^1/$_2$ pints) salted boiling water
  175 g (6 oz) plain unbleached wheat flour
  1 tbsp olive oil
  3 eggs, beaten
  ^{1}/$_2$ tsp salt and 2 tbsp fresh basil, chopped

Sieve the flour and salt onto a work surface or marble slab, and thoroughly mix in the basil. Make a well in the centre and add the oil and the eggs. Draw in the flour from the sides and gradually knead the mixture until it feels like elastic and will form into a ball. If it feels sticky, add a little more flour.

Knead the pasta for a further 10 minutes until it is shiny and smooth (if it still feels moist, knead in a small amount of flour). Cover with cling film and leave to rest at room temperature for 1 hour.

Then roll the pasta out onto a floured surface as thinly as possible – until it is almost transparent – and cut it into your preferred shapes (lasagne, tagliatelli, etc). To cook it, drop it into boiling salted water for 3 minutes, stirring occasionally. Check that it is firm, but not hard in the centre: if it isn't cooked properly it will taste raw.

This recipe makes about 225 g (^{1}/$_2$ lb) of pasta. If you want to make larger quantities, remember that you'll need to increase the amount of boiling water and salt proportionately

Filo baskets filled with garlic mushrooms

(serves 4)

For the filo baskets

110 g (4 oz) melted butter
4 x 25 cm (10 in) square sheets of filo pastry
4 x 7.5 cm (3 in) ramekin dishes (use upside down)

Preheat the oven to 180^0C/360^0F/gas mark 5. Cut each sheet of pastry into four 13 cm (5 in) squares. Brush one side of the squares with melted butter and place four sqaures (butter side down) onto each of the upside down ramekin dishes – with the last squares butter both sides. Put onto a baking tray and bake for 8-10 minutes or until golden brown. Leave to cool for a few minutes before gently lifting the baskets off the ramekins onto a wire rack.

For the mushroom filling

450 g (1 lb) flat field mushrooms (firm and pink in colour)
50 g (2 oz) unsalted butter
2 cloves of garlic, crushed
150 ml (5 fl oz) double cream
1 tbsp horseradish
1 tbsp mayonnaise (see page 30)

Wash and slice the mushrooms, and leave them to dry on some kitchen paper. Meanwhile in a shallow pan heat the butter. Add the mushrooms and gently cook for approximately 5 minutes. Strain them and leave in a warm oven-proof dish. Add the crushed garlic and the cream to the mushroom liquid, then bring back to the boil, and leave to reduce for 2 minutes or until the mixture thickens. Add the freshly ground black pepper, mushrooms, horseradish and mayonnaise, and stir in for 1 minute. Divide into the four filo baskets and sprinkle with chopped chive flowers. The filled baskets not only look good, they taste wonderful!

QUICK AND EASY SNACKS

Cornish new potato and mushroom tortilla

(serves 6)

Cornish new potatoes are often the first into the shops and so have become something quite special and eagerly looked forward to by many people.

350 g (12 oz) Cornish new potatoes, scrubbed, cooked
     and sliced
75 g (3 oz) mushrooms, sliced
1 small onion, chopped
1 tsp freshly chopped parsley
1 clove garlic, crushed
6 eggs
2 tbsp single cream
2 tbsp olive oil
salt and freshly milled black pepper

Bring a saucepan of salted water to the boil and parboil the potatoes for 5 minutes. Drain and leave to stand with the lid on. Beat the eggs in a large bowl and add the parsley and single cream. Heat the oil in a large frying pan, add the onion and cook until soft. Then put in the garlic, mushrooms and potatoes (sliced), and cook for 5 minutes or until the ingredients are turning brown.

While this process is going on, preheat the grill to a medium setting. Keeping everything in the pan, carefully pour the egg and cream mixture over the potatoes, etc.

Do not stir, but gently cook for 3 minutes or until the egg is set. Finally, place under the grill to finish off setting and browning, and then slide onto a serving dish and eat

Pan fried pizza with Devon buffalo mozzarella

(serves 6)

For the base
  225 g (8 oz) self-raising flour
  $^1/_2$ tsp salt
  1 tsp freshly chopped oregano
  1 tsp freshly milled black pepper
  2 tbsp olive oil
  5 tbsp cold water

Sieve the flour into a mixing bowl and add the other dry ingredients. Make a well in the centre and pour in the oil and the water (you may need a little more water, but don't allow the dough to become sticky). Knead the dough onto a floured board and roll out a 23 cm (9 in) circle.

You will need two shallow pans. In the first one put 1 tablespoon of olive oil, slide in the pizza base and cook gently over a low heat for about 7 minutes or until the base is golden brown. Take out, heat a second tablespoon of oil, turn the base over and cook the other side for another 7 minutes.

For the filling
  110 g (4 oz) mushrooms, sliced
  1 large onion, finely chopped
  110 g (4 oz) mixed fresh peppers, de-seeded and chopped
  1 clove garlic, crushed
  1 tsp freshly chopped parsley
  1 tsp freshly chopped marjoram
  1 tsp freshly chopped oregano
  1 tsp freshly chopped basil
  350 g (12 oz) Devon buffalo milk mozzarella cheese, grated
  3 tbsp olive oil
  3 tbsp tomato purée
  4 fresh ripe tomatoes, blanched, skinned and chopped

While the base is cooking, put 1 tablespoon of olive oil into the second pan and sauté the onion and peppers until soft. Add the garlic and mushrooms, and lastly the tomatoes and fresh herbs. Spread the base with the tomato purée and 110 g (4 oz) of cheese, then follow this with the vegetables and herbs.

Finish off with the rest of the cheese, place in the oven and cook for 5 minutes to brown at 190°C/375°F/gas mark 5.

Potato, carrot and parsnip cakes coated in herby flour

(makes 8 cakes)

225 g (8 oz) potatoes, cooked and mashed with a fork
225 g (8 oz) parsnips, lightly cooked and grated
225 g (8 oz) carrots, cooked and grated
1 tsp freshly chopped tarragon
1 tsp freshly chopped parsley
salt and freshly milled black pepper
50 g (2 oz) plain wholemeal flour, seasoned
1 egg, beaten
1 tbsp olive oil
35 g (1 oz) butter

Mix the mashed potato with the grated carrot and parsnip in a bowl, and add the seasoning and half the chopped herbs. Beat the egg separately, and in another bowl put the seasoned flour with the rest of the herbs.

Shape the vegetable mixture into 8 cakes and dip each first into the egg and then into the flour. Heat the olive oil with the butter in a shallow pan and cook the cakes for about 3 minutes per side.

Then put into the oven at 200°C/400°F/gas mark 6 for 15 minutes to cook evenly all the way through.

Pancakes

For the basic mixture (makes 12 pancakes)
    110 g (4 oz) plain flour
    2 eggs
    275 ml (½ pint) milk
    50 g (2 oz) butter

Put all the ingredients, except the butter, into a blender and blend for 1 minute. Preheat a heavy-bottomed pan about 13–18 cm (5–7 in) in size, add a knob of butter and let it melt, but not burn. Then pour in a little of the mixture and tip the pan so that it covers the base thinly. Cook for half a minute before turning the pancake and browning the other side for another half minute. Place on parchment or greaseproof paper.

With Devon Oke cheese and vegetable filling
    (this makes enough filling for 2 pancakes)
    1 clove garlic, crushed
    50 g (2 oz) mushrooms, sliced
    25 g (1 oz) shallots, chopped
    50 g (2 oz) each calabrese and cauliflower
    2 baby sweetcorn, chopped
    50 g (2 oz) Devon Oke cheddar cheese, grated
    25 g (1 oz) butter, melted

Heat 570 ml (1 pint) of water in a saucepan to boiling point and blanch the cauliflower, calabrese and baby sweetcorn for 1 minute. Then drain off the water.

Next, heat the butter in a small pan and sweat off the onions and garlic for 5 minutes until soft and without colour. Add the sliced mushrooms and cook for a further 2 minutes. Chop the remaining vegetables and stir in.

Take two pancakes, place them on a small oven-proof dish, fill with the vegetable mixture. Season, and top each with half the grated cheese and the cheese sauce.

For the delicious cheese sauce
  275 ml (10 fl oz) double cream
  75 g (3 oz) Devon oke cheddar cheese, grated

Heat the cream to boiling point and stir in the grated cheese until it melts. Pour over the pancakes, and top with slices of tomato. Bake in the oven for 10–15 minutes at 200⁰C/400⁰F/gas mark 6 until golden brown.

Creamy cheesy potatoes
  (makes 2 portions)

  225 g (8 oz) potatoes, cooked and sliced
  50 g (2 oz) cheddar cheese
  1 clove garlic, crushed
  150 ml ($1/4$ pint) single cream
  salt and milled black pepper to taste

Place half of the cooked potatoes in an oval baking dish, then add the cheese and garlic followed by the rest of the potatoes, and season. Pour the cream on top and bake in the oven at 180⁰C/360⁰F/gas mark 4 for 35 minutes.

Raw teddy fry

  2 large potatoes (teddies), peeled and irregularly sliced
  1 medium onion, sliced
  seasoning
  2 tbsp brown sauce and 1 tbsp malt vinegar
  50 g (2 oz) butter
  275 ml ($1/2$ pint) water

Melt the butter in a shallow saucepan and cook the onion for about 5 minutes until soft. Add the sliced potatoes, water, vinegar, brown sauce and seasoning, and simmer slowly without a lid for 25–30 minutes or until the teddies are cooked. This recipe must be served with thinly sliced bread and butter.

ACCOMPANIMENTS

Red cabbage braised with apples and plums
(serves 8)

This can be eaten hot or cold, and it also freezes well.

1 large red cabbage, approximately 1 kg (2 lb)
450 g (1 lb) red onions, chopped small
225 g (1/2 lb) red plums, stoned, peeled and chopped
225 g (1/2 lb) bramley apples, peeled, cored and chopped
4 tbsp dark brown sugar
4 tbsp red wine vinegar
2 fresh bay leaves
1 clove garlic, crushed (optional)
1/2 cinnamon stick
25 g (1 oz) butter
2 tbsp olive oil
sprig of thyme
milled black pepper

For this recipe you will need a 1.35 kg (3 lb) casserole dish or pan. Start by preparing the cabbage: remove the outer leaves and cut into quarters, then take out the core and shred the rest as finely as possible. Put the olive oil in the pan and heat gently. Add the chopped onions and crushed garlic, and sauté until soft and without colour. Next, put in the apples and plums, and give a good stir, followed by all the cabbage, vinegar and sugar. Cook on the stove without a lid for 5 minutes, stirring three or four times or until the sugar has dissolved.

Take off the heat and add the thyme, bay leaves, cinnamon stick and butter. Season with milled black pepper and put the lid on the pot. Transfer to the oven and cook for 2 hours at 150^{0}C/300^{0}F/gas mark 2 – give a stir about every half hour during the cooking.

Fruit, nut and Cornish Yarg coleslaw

(makes approximately 8 portions)

1 small cabbage (Dutch white)
4 spring onions
75 g (3 oz) Cornish Yarg cheese, grated
1 medium carrot, grated
25 g (1 oz) each toasted hazelnuts and toasted pecan nuts
50 g (2 oz) green seedless grapes
2 fresh ripe pears, peeled, cored and chopped
1 fresh ripe peach, skinned, stoned and chopped
freshly milled white pepper
3 tbsp mayonnaise
1 tbsp elder flower cordial

Prepare the cabbage by removing the outer leaves, cutting the cabbage into quarters and removing the core. Shred very finely into a bowl, add all the other ingredients and stir well. Chill in the fridge before serving.

Red pepper and tomato ketchup

You can make this sauce in 10 minutes.

450 g (1 lb) ripe tomatoes, chopped into small pieces
1 large red pepper, de-seeded and chopped into small pieces
2 tbsp olive oil
1 tbsp dark brown sugar
1 tbsp ginger syrup
1 tsp balsamic vinegar

Heat the oil in a saucepan and put the pepper in first. Cook for 2 minutes. Add all the other ingredients and cook for a further 5 minutes. Then put the sauce into a food processor or blender and blast for 30 seconds. Pass through a sieve and the sauce is ready to use. It will accompany most hot or cold dishes.

Blue cheese dressing

(serves 4-6)

3 tbsp mayonnaise
6 tbsp double cream
1 clove garlic
pinch of salt
1 tsp English mustard
3 tbsp olive oil
1 tbsp white wine vinegar
1 tbsp lime juice
110 g (4 oz) Somerset or Devonshire blue cheese
2 tbsp fresh chives
milled black pepper

Crush the garlic with the salt and put into a medium sized basin. Add all the other ingredients, whisk until everything is blended together and check the seasoning.

This dressing is now ready – it goes extremely well with salad or jacket potatoes.

Apple and plum chutney

(makes approximately 1.35 kg/3 lb)

450 g (1 lb) Victoria plums, blanched, peeled and stoned
225 g (8 oz) cooking apples, chopped
350 g (12 oz) shallots, chopped
1 clove garlic
725 ml (1¼ pints) white wine vinegar
350 g (12 oz) dark muscovado sugar
2 tsp salt
2 tsp mustard seeds
3 red chillies, chopped very small
2 tsp ground coriander
2 tsp ground ginger

Place the plums in a bowl and cover them with boiling water. Leave for 3 minutes and then drain – this helps to loosen the skins and makes them easier to peel. When peeled, take out the stones and chop the fruit.

Place all the ingredients into a saucepan, bring to the boil and simmer for $1^1/2$ hours by which time the chutney should be of a pulpy consistency. Leave to stand for 20 minutes before transferring to sterilised jars.

Seal and leave for 1 month to give the flavours time to mature.

Spicy tomato sauce

>   2 large onions, chopped
>   900 g (2 lb) very ripe tomatoes, blanched, peeled and
>   chopped
>   2 cloves garlic, crushed
>   2 tbsp olive oil
>   2 tbsp soy sauce
>   1 tbsp dark brown sugar
> $1/2$ tsp ground cumin
> $1/2$ tsp ground coriander
> $1/4$ tsp chilli powder

Blanch the tomatoes in boiling water for 30 seconds or until you see their skins beginning to come away. Plunge into cold water and peel.

Using a fairly large saucepan heat the olive oil and sauté the onions and garlic until soft and without colour. Add the chopped tomatoes and the rest of the ingredients (be sparing with the spices if you don't like things too 'hot'), and cook gently for 15–20 minutes or until you have a sauce consistency.

Balsamic glaze

275 ml (10 fl oz) balsamic vinegar
175 g (6 oz) dark muscovado sugar

A very useful glaze to have in your fridge. It complements sweet and savoury dishes such as cheesecakes, pear and champagne ice cream, salads, pasta, etc.

In a shallow pan place the two ingredients and gently bring to the boil, stirring all the time until the sugar has dissolved and the liquid is of a syrupy consistency. Pour into a jar and use when needed.

Mayonnaise

3 egg yolks
425 ml ($^3/_4$ pt) olive oil
1 tsp mustard
$^1/_4$ tsp salt
8 turns freshly ground black pepper
2 tbsp cider vinegar
2 tbsp lemon juice

Place all the ingredients, except the olive oil, into a liquidiser. Turn onto the lowest speed and trickle in the oil. When the mixture starts to thicken, you can turn the speed up one notch and trickle a little faster.

If you think the mayonnaise is too thick, just add a few drops of luke warm water until it suits the consistency you require.

VEGETABLE STOCK

This recipe makes 2.25 litres (4 pints).

    4 large onions, finely chopped
    2 large carrots, roughly chopped
    2 leeks, finely chopped
    2 fennel bulbs, finely chopped
    2 stalks celery, chopped
    chervil and parsley stalks
    1 fresh bay leaf
    12 whole peppercorns
    2 cloves garlic, chopped
    2.25 litres (4 pints) cold water

Place all the vegetables and the water in a large pan, and bring to the boil – leaving the lid off. Turn down the heat and simmer for 15 minutes. Then remove from the stove, and strain through a fine sieve – use the back of a ladle to force the liquid through into a bowl.

If you're not going to use the stock immediately, you can store it in your fridge for up to 5 days or, if you freeze it, for up to a month.

PUDDINGS

Lemon brûlée tart

For the pastry
  350 g (12 oz) plain flour, sifted
  225 g (8 oz) butter, chopped
  4 tbsp ice cold water

Put the flour and butter into a blender or food processor and blend for 5 seconds. Then pulse in the water until a ball has formed. Refrigerate for 30 minutes.

Grease 6 individual fluted tart tins (10 cm/4 in wide and 4 cm/1^1/$_2$ in deep)and line them with the rolled out pastry. Chill for a further 10 minutes, then put a piece of greaseproof paper and baking beans on each of them and bake blind for 15 minutes at 200⁰C/400⁰F/gas mark 6. When the pastry is beginning to brown but is not quite ready, take off the beans and paper and put back in the oven for another 5 minutes. Keep checking, as the pastry will brown very quickly!

For the filling (this is better made the day before)
  1 lemon, grated and squeezed (aim for 2 tbsp juice)
  8 egg yolks
  110 g (4 oz) caster sugar
  570 ml (1 pint) double cream

Heat the cream in a saucepan to nearly boiling point. Whisk the egg yolks and sugar together until double in size and very pale in colour. Carefully add the hot cream, and stir gently.

Make a bain marie by placing a saucepan with about a third of water on the cooker on a low heat and putting the bowl with the brûlée mixture into the pan.

Keep whisking from time to time until the mixture thickens. This can take around half an hour, so maintain a watchful eye and be patient, but don't leave it too long or it might curdle!

When thick enough, add the lemon rind and juice. Test for

taste, as lemons do vary in strength and juiciness, but remember the flavour will become stronger. Leave to cool and place in the fridge to set. It is then ready to fill the pastry cases.

Dust with icing sugar and pop under the grill for a few seconds (some people use a blow torch for this job). Put back in the fridge for a few minutes to crisp up the sugar and to give the brûlée time to reset. It is then ready to serve.

Devonshire apple and nutmeg bread and butter pudding
(serves 8)

12 slices of bread buttered each side (remove the crusts and cut each slice into 4 triangles)
450 (1 lb) bramley apples, puréed
75 g (3 oz) muscovado sugar, plus 25 g (1 oz) for sprinkling on the top
1 lemon, rind and juice
1 orange, rind and juice
4 eggs, beaten
275 ml (1/2 pint) single cream
1/2 tsp freshly grated nutmeg

In a 1.2 litre (2 pint) round oven-proof dish place a third of the prepared bread over the bottom. Spread with half of the apple purée and half the freshly grated nutmeg.

Whisk together the eggs, sugar, orange and lemon rinds and juice in a mixing bowl, and cover the first layer of the pudding with a third of the liquid.

Repeat the process once more and finish with the rest of the liquid. Sprinkle with sugar.

Leave to stand in the refrigerator for 1 hour before baking in a preheated oven (190°C/375°F/gas mark 5) for 1 hour.

West Country Christmas pudding

(makes 2 puddings)

110 g (4 oz) carrot, grated
110 g (4 oz) apple, grated
110 g (4 oz) butter, melted
110 g (4 oz) dark brown muscovado sugar
110 g (4 oz) raisins
110 g (4 oz) currants
110 g (4 oz) sultanas
50 g (2 oz) chopped figs
110 g (4 oz) chopped candied peel
225 g (8 oz) fresh white bread crumbs
50 g (2 oz) almonds, chopped (leave their skins on)
50 g (2 oz) brazil nuts, chopped
25 g (1 oz) pine kernels (do not chop)
2 lemons, grated and squeezed
3 size 2 eggs, beaten
1 tbsp black treacle
2 tbsp clear honey
2 tbsp medium sherry (optional)
50 g (2 oz) self-raising flour
50 g (2 oz) ground almonds
1 tsp mixed spice
$^1/_2$ tsp cinnamon
$^1/_2$ tsp baking powder
pinch of salt

Sieve together in a large bowl the flour, cinnamon, mixed spice, salt, baking powder and ground almonds. Add the sugar, bread crumbs, fruit, chopped nuts, pine kernels and grated apple and carrot.

In a second bowl measure out the black treacle and honey, and mix in the melted butter, sherry, eggs, and lemon rind and juice. Add to the dry ingredients and stir well.

Butter two 1 litre (2 pint) pudding basins and three-quarters fill each. Cover with parchment paper, followed by tin foil, and steam for 4 hours or longer if preferred. On the day you want to eat the pudding, steam for at least another 2 hours and serve with brandy or rum sauce, or clotted cream.

For the brandy or rum sauce

50 g (2 oz) butter   40 g (1 1/2 oz) plain flour
50 g (2 oz) caster sugar   570 ml (1 pint) milk
150 ml (1/4 pint) double cream   3 tbsp brandy or rum

Using a small saucepan, melt the butter slowly, then add the flour and stir with a wooden spoon until smooth. Gradually pour in the milk, whisking well each time to free the mixture from any lumps. When all the milk has been incorporated, you should have a smooth and creamy consistency. Turn the heat down as low as possible, add the sugar and cook for 5 minutes, stirring all the time to prevent any sticking. When ready, add your chosen spirit and the cream, and serve.

Cider syllabub

(makes 6)

A delicious light creamy dessert best served with home-made sponge fingers (see page 41).

170 ml (6 fl oz) West Country cider
275 ml (1/2 pint) double cream
50 g (2 oz) caster sugar
2 tbsp freshly squeezed lemon juice

Put the sugar, lemon juice and cider into a mixing bowl and whisk for a few minutes until the sugar has dissolved. Then gradually whisk in the cream until the mixture thickens. Spoon into six stem glasses and top each with lemon zest. Place in the fridge for at least 3 hours.

Cornish Yarg and plum pie

(serves 6)

For the pastry

350 g (12 oz) plain flour
pinch of salt
1 tbsp caster sugar
$1/2$ tsp ground cinnamon
175 g (6 oz) butter
1 egg yolk
4 tbsp ice cold water

For the filling

450 g (1 lb) ripe plums, stoned and sliced
175 g (6 oz) Cornish Yarg cheese, chopped
1 tsp chopped pineapple mint (optional)
2 tbsp muscovado sugar
egg to glaze

Firstly, sift the flour, salt and cinnamon into a bowl, then stir in the sugar and rub in the butter. When the mixture resembles fine bread crumbs, add the egg yolk and water to form a soft dough. Wrap in cling film and put into the fridge for 20 minutes to chill.

Heat the oven to 200°C/400°F/gas mark 6. Roll out half the pastry and line a 20 cm (8 in) round sponge tin. Place some greaseproof paper and baking beans on top, and bake blind for 10 minutes. After removing the paper and beans, fill with all the remaining ingredients.

Roll out the other half of the pastry and cover the top of the pie. Brush with egg glaze and cook for 35–40 minutes or until golden brown. Serve while still warm.

Sweet short crust pastry

  225 g (8 oz) plain flour
  150 g (5 oz) butter, cut into small cubes
  1 tsp caster sugar
  1 whole egg, beaten with 1–3 tbsp ice cold water
  pinch of salt

Sift the flour into a mixing bowl. Make a well in the centre and add the salt and the sugar. Rub in the butter until it feels like sand between your finger tips.

Add the liquid (egg and water) and mix to a dough. If this isn't enough liquid, just add a little more water a drop at a time – but don't make the dough too wet.

Wrap in clingfilm and refrigerate for 45 minutes. This is a must, as pastry has to relax and firm up before you use it.

When rolling, use plenty of flour so that it doesn't stick to your board – this pastry is not always the easiest to handle. It works well with the lemon brûlée tart recipe on page 32.

Rhubarb sorbet

  450 g (1 lb) fresh young rhubarb, chopped
  450 g (1 lb) granulated sugar
  570 ml (1 pt) cold water

Place all the ingredients into a saucepan and bring to the boil. Simmer for approximately 10 minutes until the rhubarb is cooked. Take off the heat and leave until cold.

Then put in a food processor for 30 seconds, and pour into an ice cream maker and churn for 20 minutes.

If you don't have an ice cream maker, put into a freezer-proof container, freeze for 1 hour, take out and give it a good beating. Repeat the process 3 more times.

Somerset apple and almond cheesecake

For the filling
    225 g (8 oz) cream cheese
    275 m (1/2 pt) double cream
    275 ml (1/2 pt) Yeo Valley natural organic yoghurt
    50 g (2 oz) caster sugar
    225 g (8 oz) apple purée
    1 tsp almond extract (adjust to suit your taste)
    1 tsp gelatine mixed with 3 tbsp water

In a saucepan bring the cream and sugar to boiling point, stirring all the time or until the sugar has dissolved. Take off the heat and add the prepared gelatine, again stirring until it has dissolved. Leave to cool for 5 minutes.

In a separate bowl mix the cream cheese with the yoghurt and fold in the apple purée. Add the almond essence and fold into the cream mixture.

Then pour into a lined 20 cm/8 in round, loose-bottomed tin, and put in the fridge for approximately 45 minutes to set.

For the biscuit base
    225 g (8 oz) Amaretti biscuits, crushed
    80 g (3 1/2 oz) melted butter

Mix the ingredients together and spoon over the cheese cake. Cover with cling film and put back in the fridge for 30 minutes. Turn out onto a flat plate, decorate with a little whipped cream and fresh raspberries, and serve with raspberry coulis.

Raspberry coulis

225 g (8 oz) fresh raspberries
25 g (1 oz) icing sugar
2 tbsp freshly squeezed lemon juice
1 tbsp cold water

Place all the ingredients into a food processor and whiz for 30 seconds. Strain through a very fine sieve.

Blackberry and apple ice cream

225 g (8 oz) prepared sliced cooking apple
50 g (2 oz) caster sugar
175 g (6 oz) blackberries

For the custard
4 egg yolks
125 g (4 oz) caster sugar
175 ml (6 fl oz) double cream
175 ml (6 fl oz) full fat milk

Cook the apple with 50 g (2 oz) of sugar and the blackberries in a saucepan for 10 minutes or until soft.

Heat the cream and milk, and bring to boiling point. Place the egg yolks and the remaining sugar in a food mixer and whisk until light and fluffy.

Turn down to a low speed and add the cream and milk. Whisk gently until fully incorporated, then place back onto a very low heat, stirring all the time with a spatula until the mixture reaches 84^{0}C.

Take off the heat and add the blackberry and apple. Leave to stand until cold, then pour into an ice cream maker and churn for 20 minutes. Or put in a freezer-proof container for 1 hour, take out and whisk. Repeat this process 4 times.

Pear, cinnamon and Camel Valley
sparkling wine ice cream

450 g (1 lb) prepared conference pears
1 bottle Camel Valley sparkling wine
2 cinnamon sticks
quantity of ice cream custard as for apple and blackberry ice
    cream (page 39)

Place the pears, wine and cinnamon sticks in a large saucepan and bring to the boil. Turn down the heat and simmer until the pears are transparent – approximately 20 minutes (sometimes they take a bit longer to cook depending on how ripe they are).

Take off the heat and, when cool enough, place in a food processor and whiz for about a minute or until everything is a smooth purée. Add to the ice cream custard and repeat as for blackberry and apple ice cream.

CAKES AND BISCUITS

Cornish shortbread

200 g (7 oz) butter
225 g (8 oz) plain flour
110 g (2 oz) rice flour
110 g (2 oz) caster sugar
pinch of salt
$^1/_2$ tsp ground cinnamon

Place all the ingredients together in a blender or food processor and blend for about 20 seconds until the mixture resembles very fine bread crumbs. Then pulse two or three times.

Transfer to a bowl and push together with your hands to form a soft ball.

Lightly dust a board with caster sugar and roll out the paste quickly and lightly to 1 cm ($^1/_2$ in) thick. Put into a 200 cm (8 in) flan tin, make a finger indentation around the edge and prick with a fork before baking in the oven at 150⁰C/300⁰F/gas mark 2 for 1 hour or until golden brown in colour.

After you've taken the shortbread out of the oven, cut into biscuit shapes straight away. Leave to cool before lifting them from the tin with a pallet knife and dredging with caster sugar.

Sponge fingers
(makes 24)

125 g (4 oz) plain flour, sieved
4 eggs, separated
125 g (4 oz) caster sugar
1 tsp vanilla essence
icing sugar for sprinkling
pinch of salt
piping bag with a 2 cm ($^3/_4$ in) nozzle

Whisk the egg yolks, vanilla essence and sugar together until light and fluffy. Fold in very carefully the sieved flour and salt. Next whisk the egg whites until stiff and, with a metal spoon, fold in one tablespoon of this to relax the mixture. Then fold in the rest with the metal spoon, again taking care.

Cover two baking trays with parchment. Fill the piping bag with the mixture and pipe 11 cm (4$^{1}/_{2}$ in) long fingers 10 cm (4 in) apart. Dust with the icing sugar and bake in the oven for 15–18 minutes at 175^{0}C/350^{0}F/gas mark 4. Remove and cool on a wire rack.

Kay's Cornish carrot and coconut cake

175 g (6 oz) grated carrot
2 eggs
110 g (4 oz) dark brown muscovado sugar
75 ml (3 fl oz) oil
50 g (2 oz) desiccated coconut
110 g (4 oz) self-raising wholemeal flour
50 g (2 oz) sultanas
$^{1}/_{2}$ tsp salt
1 tsp cinnamon

Preheat the oven to 180^{0}C/350^{0}F/gas mark 4. Then grease and line a 450 g (1 lb) loaf tin with parchment paper. Beat the eggs and the sugar together before adding the oil, drop by drop.

Sieve the flour, salt and cinnamon together and gradually fold into the mixture, alternating with the carrot, coconut and sultanas. Put the cake mixture into the prepared tin and bake for 1–1$^{1}/_{4}$ hours.

Savoury potato and Cornish Yarg cheese scones

(makes 12 scones)

110 g (4 oz) potatoes, boiled and mashed
225 g (8 oz) self-raising flour
50 g (2 oz) Cornish Yarg cheese, grated
50 g (2 oz) butter
$^{1}/_{2}$ tsp salt
pinch cayenne pepper
75 ml (3 fl oz) milk

Preheat the oven to 190⁰C/375⁰F/gas mark 5 and line a baking tray with parchment paper.

Sieve the flour and salt together into a bowl and rub in the butter until the mixture resembles fine bread crumbs. Add the cheese, mashed potato and milk, and mix together to form a soft dough.

Roll out onto a floured board to 1.5 cm ($^{1}/_{2}$ in) in thickness and cut with a 5 cm (2 in) cutter. Place onto the baking tray and cook for 10–15 minutes or until golden brown.

Cornish ginger fairings

75 g (3 oz) butter
75 g (3 oz) caster sugar
3 tbsp golden syrup
175 g (6 oz) plain flour
$^{1}/_{4}$ tsp salt
1 tsp bicarbonate of soda
1 tsp baking powder
$^{1}/_{2}$ tsp cinnamon
1 tsp mixed spice
2 tsp ground ginger

Line two baking trays with parchment paper. Measure the syrup into a basin and stand in a saucepan of hot water to warm the syrup before use.

Sieve the flour, baking powder, salt, bicarbonate of soda and spices, and rub in the butter. Add the sugar and warm syrup, and mix in thoroughly.

Rub flour onto your hands before rolling the mixture into small balls, about the size of a 2-pence coin or roughly 10 g ($^1/_2$ oz) in weight.

Place on the baking trays, allowing room for the biscuits to spread, and put on the top shelf of the oven at 180⁰C/350⁰F/gas mark 4 for 15 minutes or until nicely browned.

Somerset apple, honey and pecan nut cake

175 g (6 oz) self-raising flour
1 tbsp baking powder
75 g (3 oz) butter (at room temperature)
75 g (3 oz) caster sugar
2 x size 2 fresh free-range eggs
75 g (3 oz) diced cooking apple
50 g (2 oz) ground almonds
50 g (2 oz) pecan nuts, chopped
2 tbsp clear honey
2 tbsp milk
$^1/_4$ tsp salt

For the topping
75 g (3 oz) dark muscovado sugar
75 g (3 oz) self-raising flour
75 g (3 oz) chopped pecan nuts
50 g (2 oz) butter
1 tbsp apple juice

Make the topping first and leave to one side. Sieve the flour, add the sugar and rub in the butter. Add the nuts and lastly mix altogether with the apple juice.

Line a 20 cm (8 in) round, loose-bottomed cake tin with

parchment or greaseproof paper. In a large mixing bowl sieve the flour, baking powder and salt. Add the ground almonds and sugar, and mix together thoroughly. Rub in the soft butter, add the nuts and apple, and then fold in the eggs, milk and the honey.

Place into the prepared tin. Spoon over the topping and bake in a moderate oven (180⁰C/360⁰F/gas mark 5) for 45 minutes.

Do not remove from the baking tin for 25 minutes. Turn out onto a wire rack and eat either hot, with some delicious toffee sauce, or cold, with a good cup of afternoon tea.

Toffee sauce

  100g (4 oz) unsalted butter
  275 ml ($1/2$ pint) double cream
  175 g (6 oz) dark muscovado sugar
  $1/2$ tsp vanilla extract

In a saucepan over a gentle heat melt the butter. Then add the sugar, stirring continually until the sugar has dissolved (about 3 to 4 minutes). Add the cream and whisk. Take off the heat and the sauce is ready to serve.

Somerset yoghurt and citrus cake

Grease and line 2 x 450 g (1 lb) loaf tins

  Use the tub as your scales
  225 g (8 oz) Yeo Valley organic yoghurt
  1 tub sunflower oil
  $1^1/2$ tubs caster sugar
  3 tubs self-raising flour
  3 eggs
  1 lemon, grated and squeezed
  1 lime, grated and squeezed

Using an electric mixer, whisk the eggs and sugar together to ribbon stage. Then turn the speed down to slow and gradually add the oil and zest of the fruit. Lastly, fold in the flour alternately with the yoghurt and citrus juice.

Now divide the mixture between the prepared tins and bake in a moderate oven (180°C/350°F/gas mark 4) for approximately 45 minutes.

For the citrus icing
    225 g (8 oz) icing sugar
    1 lemon, grated and squeezed
    1 lime, grated and squeezed

In a mixing bowl sift the icing sugar. Add the zest and juice until the mixture is smooth. Then, when the cakes are cool, pour the icing over the top and leave until firm.

Some other books about West Country food

Clotted Cream, Carolyn Martin (Tor Mark)
Traditions and recipes for one of the West Country's most
distinctive products.

The Herb Book, Deborah Fowler & Sally Cuckson (Truran)
A simple, straightforward guide to growing, preserving and
cooking with popular herbs based on practical experience.

Fish Recipes from the South West, Heather Corbett (Tor Mark)
Very tasty recipes that are extremely easy to prepare.

Pasties and cream, Hettie Merrick (Truran)
A collection of reminiscences and recipes from a Cornish
childhood in the 1930s and 1940s.

Pasty Book, Hettie Merrick (Tor Mark)
Hettie Merrick for many years ran a pasty shop at the Lizard.
Here she describes pasty traditions and provides a variety of
recipes.

Traditional Devon Recipes, Carolyn Martin (Bossiney Books)
An expert food researcher pools the wisdom of cooks across
the centuries to bring the best of the county's traditions to the
modern kitchen.

Traditional Somerset Recipes, Carolyn Martin (Bossiney Books)
Tempt family and friends with the delights of cheese soup,
whitpit, Taunton toast, crocky pie, apple dappy, rhubarb tansy,
frumenty, Sally Lunns, Colston buns and Cattern cakes.

INDEX OF RECIPES